I0171438

Cover and interior illustrations by Davor Ratkovic
Printed in the United States of America

MIXING TABLE

If you want to experiment, this table can help you :-)

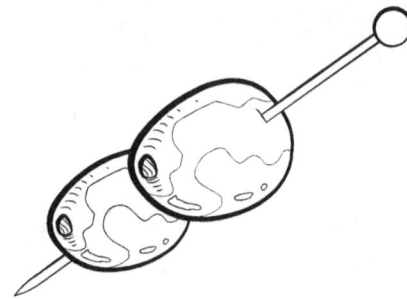

	Vermouth	Campari	Champagne	Gin	Vodka	Rum	Tequila	Cognac	Whiskey (bourbon)	Cointreau/Curacao	Malibu	Apricot Brandy	Coffee liqueur	Cherry liqueur	Fruit juice	Lemonade	Coke
Vermouth	■	✓	O	✓	✓	O	O	O	✓	✓	✗	✗	✗	O	O	✗	✗
Campari	✓	■	✓	✓	✓	✗	✗	✗	✗	✓	✗	✗	✗	✗	✓	✓	✗
Champagne	O	✓	■	O	✗	O	✗	✓	O	✓	✗	O	✗	O	✓	✗	✗
Gin	✓	✓	O	■	✗	✗	✗	✗	✗	✓	O	✓	✗	✓	✓	✓	✓
Vodka	✓	✓	✗	✗	■	✗	✗	✗	✗	✓	✓	✓	✓	✓	✓	✓	✓
Rum	O	✗	O	✗	✗	■	✗	✗	✗	✓	✓	✓	✓	✓	✓	✓	✓
Tequila	O	✗	✗	✗	✗	✗	■	✗	✗	✓	✓	✓	✓	✓	✓	✓	✓
Cognac	O	✗	✓	✗	✗	✗	✗	■	✗	✓	✓	✓	✓	✓	✓	O	✓
Whiskey (bourbon)	✓	✗	O	✗	✗	✗	✗	✗	■	✓	O	O	O	✓	✓	✓	✓
Cointreau/Curacao	O	✓	✓	✓	✓	✓	✓	✓	✓	■	O	O	O	O	✓	✓	O
Malibu	✗	✗	✗	O	✓	✓	✓	✓	O	O	■	O	O	O	✓	✓	✗
Apricot Brandy	✗	✗	O	✓	✓	✓	✓	✓	O	O	O	■	O	O	✓	O	✗
Coffee liqueur	✗	✗	✗	✗	✓	✓	✓	✓	O	O	O	O	■	O	✓	✗	✗
Cherry liqueur	O	✗	O	✓	✓	✓	✓	✓	✓	O	O	O	O	■	✓	✓	O
Fruit juice	O	✓	✓	✓	✓	✓	✓	✓	✓	✓	✓	✓	✓	✓	■	O	✗
Lemonade	✗	✓	✗	✓	✓	✓	✓	O	✓	✓	✓	O	✗	✓	O	■	✗
Coke	✗	✗	✗	✓	✓	✓	✓	✓	✓	O	✗	✗	✗	O	✗	✗	■

✓ Great Pairing

✗ Not So Much

O Optional (in smaller doses)

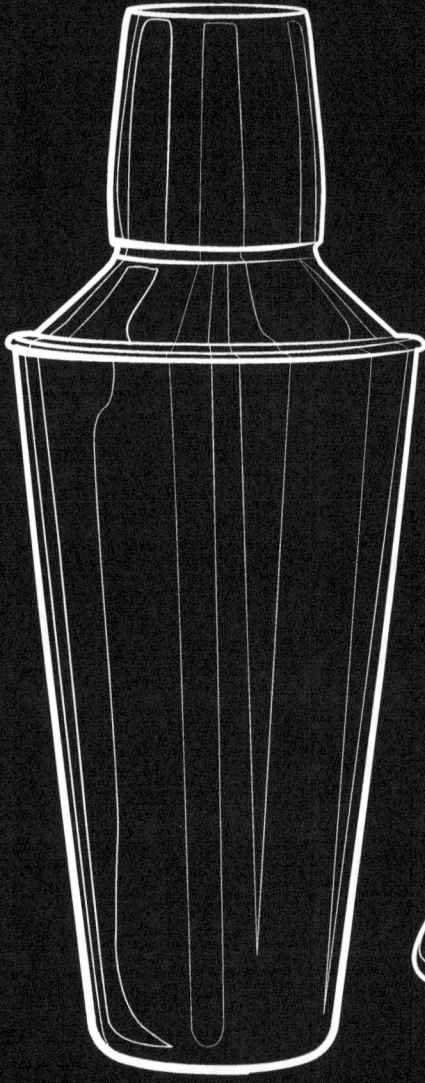

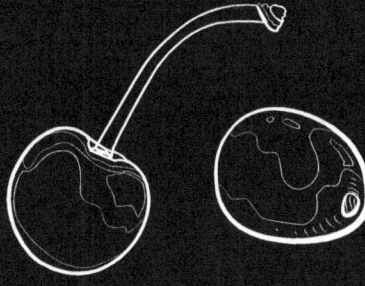

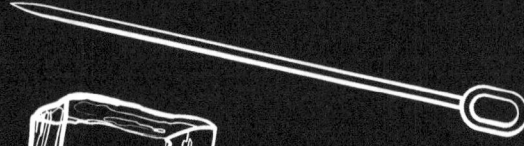

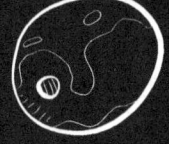

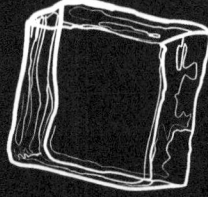

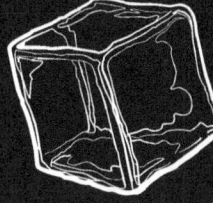

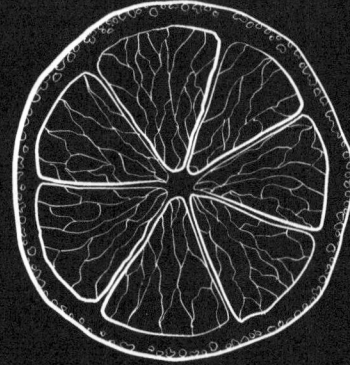

Crushed
Ice

Ice
Cubes

Ice Cube
to cool
down

Shaker

Stir

Blender

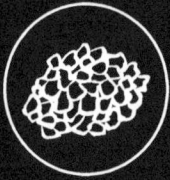

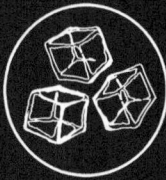

Collins
highball
glass

Bowl
glass

Old
Fashioned
glass

Coffee
glass / mug

Cocktail
glass

Hurricane
glass

BOURBON

Timing: After dinner

Old Fashioned glass

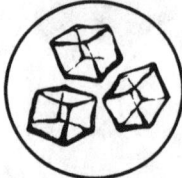
Ice Cubes

Stir

INGREDIENTS:

>>> 1/2 teaspoon sugar
>>> 3 dashes Angostura bitters
>>> 1 teaspoon water
>>> 2 ounces bourbon

Garnish: orange peel

PREPARATION:

Add the water, bitters, and sugar, into a rocks glass, then stir until sugar is dissolved.
Fill up the glass with big ice cubes, then add in the bourbon, and stir gently.
Squeeze your orange peel up over the glass, then drop it in.

The original cocktail. The Old Fashioned fits the very definition of cocktail as it was first described in 1806.
As more cocktails were created, a bartender knew exactly what you meant when you asked for a cocktail made "in the old fashioned way".
It was good enough for Don Draper and conjures images of leather upholstery and green felt table tops in smoky, boozy atmospheres.

Old Fashioned

GIN

Timing: Before dinner

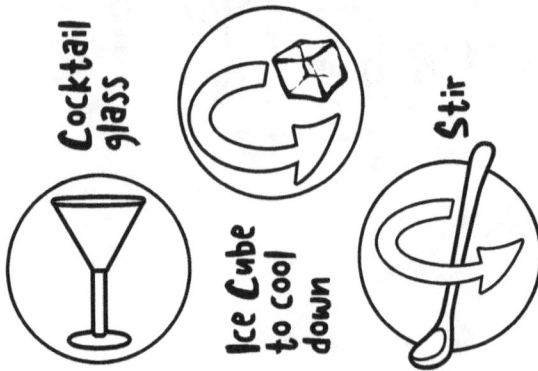

Cocktail glass

Ice Cube to cool down

Stir

INGREDIENTS:

>>> 2 1/2 ounces gin
>>> 1/2 ounce dry vermouth
>>> 1 dash orange bitters (optional)

Garnish: Olives or lemon twist

PREPARATION:

Add everything into mixing glass with ice and then stir until it's very, very cold. (Never shake!)
Strain it into a chilled martini (cocktail) glass. Add garnish.

Here's something weird about martinis. There was a martini glass BEFORE there was a drink called the martini.
Even more confusing, bartenders today often serve martinis in coupettes. Regardless, a martini deserves to be served in a glass with a long stem so that it does not warm up too quickly.
The wide brim increases air exposure which brings out flavor and the steep sides help support the olive skewer and keep the ingredients from separating.
The perfect drink seems to have been invented just to fit the glass.

Dry MarTini

RUM

Timing: All day

Hurricane glass

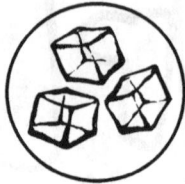

Ice Cubes

Blender

INGREDIENTS:

>>> 2 ounces light rum
>>> 1 1/2 ounces cream of coconut
>>> 1 1/2 ounces pineapple juice
>>> 1/2 ounce lime juice,
     freshly squeezed

Garnish: pineapple wedge,
     pineapple leaf

PREPARATION:

Feel free to toss everything into a blender with ice but you can also simply shake with ice and strain for a slightly deconstructed version.

Add everything to your shaker full of ice and shake for 20-30 seconds.

Strain into chilled Hurricane glass over fresh ice.

Garnish with pineapple leaf and pineapple wedge.

Here we have the national drink of Puerto Rico! In Spanish, it literally means pineapple (piña) strained (colada). The fun legend of this drink's origin is that the Caribbean pirate, Roberto Cofresi, would serve it to his crew to keep them happy and avoid mutinous inclinations which seems quite clever of him. I'm guessing he didn't serve them frozen, with frilly cocktail umbrellas in fancy glasses.

RUM

Timing: After dinner

Cocktail glass

Crushed Ice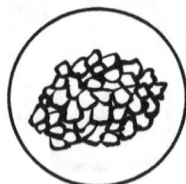

Shaker

INGREDIENTS:

>>> 1/2 lime (juiced)
>>> 1 1/4 ounces orange juice
>>> 1 ounce light rum
>>> 1 ounce dark rum
>>> 1/4 ounce Galliano Liqueur

Garnish: maraschino cherry, lemon, sprig of mint

PREPARATION:

Squeeze the lime juice into your shaker with ice.
Add the rum, orange juice, and the Galliano and shake for 10-15 seconds. Strain into a Coctail glass over fresh crushed ice. Add your garnish.

Here is another tiki inspired cocktail of the Caribbean.
It's name likely comes from the Haitian folk song made popular by Harry Belafonte in the late 50's. It is a song of longing and even despair.
"Wish that I were a yellow bird, I'd fly away with you. But I am not a yellow bird, so here I sit. Nothing I can do. Yellow bird, yellow bird."
Fortunately the drink is sunny and full of cheer!

Yellow Bird

VODKA

Timing: All day

Hurricane glass

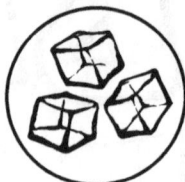

Ice Cubes

Shaker

INGREDIENTS:

>>> 1 1/2 ounces vodka
>>> 1/2 ounce peach schnapps
>>> 1 1/2 ounces orange or
　　　pineapple juice
>>> 1 1/2 ounces cranberry juice
>>> 1/2 ounce Chambord or
　　　crème de cassis (optional)

Garnish: cocktail umbrella for the win

PREPARATION:

Add everything to a shaker with ice and shake for 10-15 seconds.
Strain into a hurricane or highball glass over fresh ice. Toss in a cocktail umbrella if you're feeling cheeky.

Easy to drink and easy to make, this naughtily named cocktail was made for a group of people that really needed no help at all at loosening up...Florida Spring breakers. The year was 1987. The place was none other than Fort Lauderdale, Florida. Whoa momma!
A promotion by a peach schnapps company inspired bartender Ted Pizio to try and win $1000 by selling the most over Spring Break. He named the drink after the two things Spring breakers love the most. Nobody keeps it classy like Fort Lauderdale!

Sex on the Beach

HARD MIX

Timing: After dinner

Collins glass

Ice Cubes

Stir

INGREDIENTS:

>>> 3/4 oz Vodka
>>> 3/4 oz White rum
>>> 3/4 oz Silver tequila
>>> 3/4 oz Gin
>>> 3/4 oz Triple sec
>>> 3/4 oz Simple syrup
>>> 3/4 oz Fresh lemon juice
>>> Coke, to top

Garnish: Lemon wedge

PREPARATION:

No fancy shaking here!
Pour everything except the Coke into a Collins glass over ice.
Top with a splash of Coke and stir.
Garnish with lemon wedge.

Aaah, do you remember your very first sip of a Long Island Iced Tea?
Of course not! Nobody does!
It has FIVE shots of FIVE different white liquors in it.
Whether it was invented on an island in a Tennessee river in the 20's or in the 60's during a bartending contest in the ritzy Hamptons area of Long Island, NY, it was designed for one thing and one thing only...
to have a rip roarin' good time.

RUM

Timing: After dinner

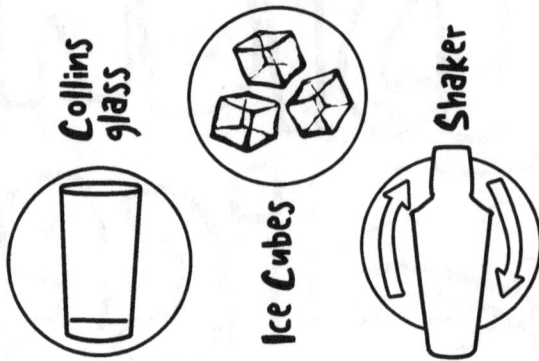

Collins glass

Ice Cubes

Shaker

INGREDIENTS:

>>> 2 ounces Gosling's Black Seal rum (or replacement rum of your choice)
>>> 1/2 ounce lime juice, freshly squeezed
>>> ginger beer, to top (about 5 ounces)

Garnish: lime wedge

PREPARATION:

Pour the rum and the lime juice into a tall glass over ice.
Top with your ginger beer.
Add garnish.

This is the cocktail of seafarers the world over but originates from Bermuda, the shipwreck capital of the world due to its dangerous coral reef. As legend has it, the cocktail gets its name from an old sailor who compared the drink's dark color to that of storm clouds.
Sailors do have an eye for both stormy skies and good cocktails...

Dark 'n' Stormy

VODKA

Timing: All day

Collins glass

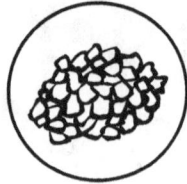

Crushed Ice

Shaker gently

PREPARATION:

Lightly mash or muddle the mint in the shaker. Pour in the rum, the lime juice, the simple syrup, fill with ice and shake for just a few seconds.
Strain into a Collins glass over crushed ice. Top with club soda. Add your garnish.

One of the oldest mixed drinks that you can make, the Mojito is over 500 years old and comes to us from Cuba. Pirates actually drank an early version to treat dysentery and scurvy. Why would you just eat limes when you can drink rum with it? Crafty pirates...this drink was also a favorite of Ernest Heminway. While Ernest didn't encounter too many drinks he didn't like, his old standby was the mojito. It's certainly hard to be uptight with a mojito in your hand. So whether you suffer from scurvy or anxiety, let's get that fixed shall we?

CACHAÇA

Timing: After dinner

Old Fashioned glass

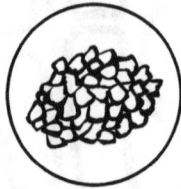
Crushed Ice

Stir

INGREDIENTS:

>>> 1 1/2 limes, cut into wedges
>>> 2 tsp sugar
>>> 2 ounces cachaça (aged rum makes a decent substitute but you'll want to try cachaca)

Garnish: lime wheel

PREPARATION:

In a Rocks glass (old fashioned), muddle or mash the lime with the sugar.
Fill it up with crashed ice, add in the cachaça, and stir.
Garnish with lime wheel, put on a bathing suit, and find a pool to drink by.

The national cocktail of Brazil, the Caipirinha is a fun drink to make. But let's start with pronunciation. Kai-Pur-EEN-Ya. It's made with Brazil's favorite liquor, Cachaca. It's in the same ballpark as rum, but distilled directly from sugarcane rather than molasses like rum is. Pronounced Ka-SHAH-Suh. That's a funny one isn't it? It's actually the 3rd most consumed spirit worldwide.
This drink is mouth wateringly refreshing and sure to impress your friends as this popular drink is probably not one they've ever heard of, much less able to pronounce. Not quite a margarita, not quite a mojito, you'll just have to try it yourself.

Timing: Mid-afternoon

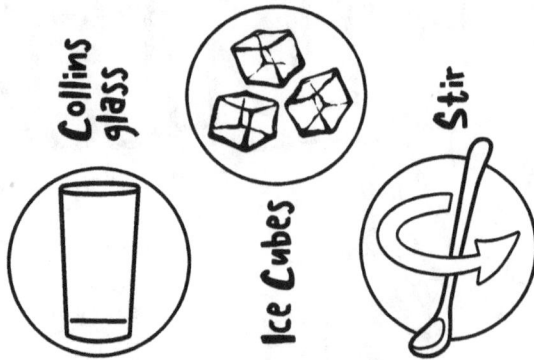

Collins glass

Ice Cubes

Stir

INGREDIENTS:

>>> 1 1/2 ounces
   Tennessee whiskey
>>> 1 ounce triple sec
>>> 1 ounce lemon juice
>>> Ice
>>> 4 ounces lemon-lime soda

Garnish: Lemon wheels or slices

PREPARATION:

First pour the lemon juice, triple sec and most importantly the Jack Daniels into a Collins glass (or mason jar) and add ice.
Top with the lemon-lime soda.
Stir and add in some lemon slices.
Easy peasy lemon squeezy.

The year was 1980. It was the wild west of cocktail invention.
The inventor of this drink was Tony Mason, an Alabama restaurateur who claimed the recipe was then stolen by a Jack Daniels sales rep. Jack Daniels promoted the drink and it did really well. After a long legal battle, the restaurateur won the case! Unfortunately, he was awarded no money. The judge offered him $1 which he rejected. Ouch.

Lynchburg Lemonade

GIN

Timing: After dinner

Highball glass

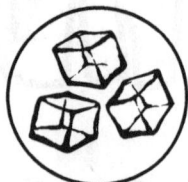
Ice Cubes

Shaker

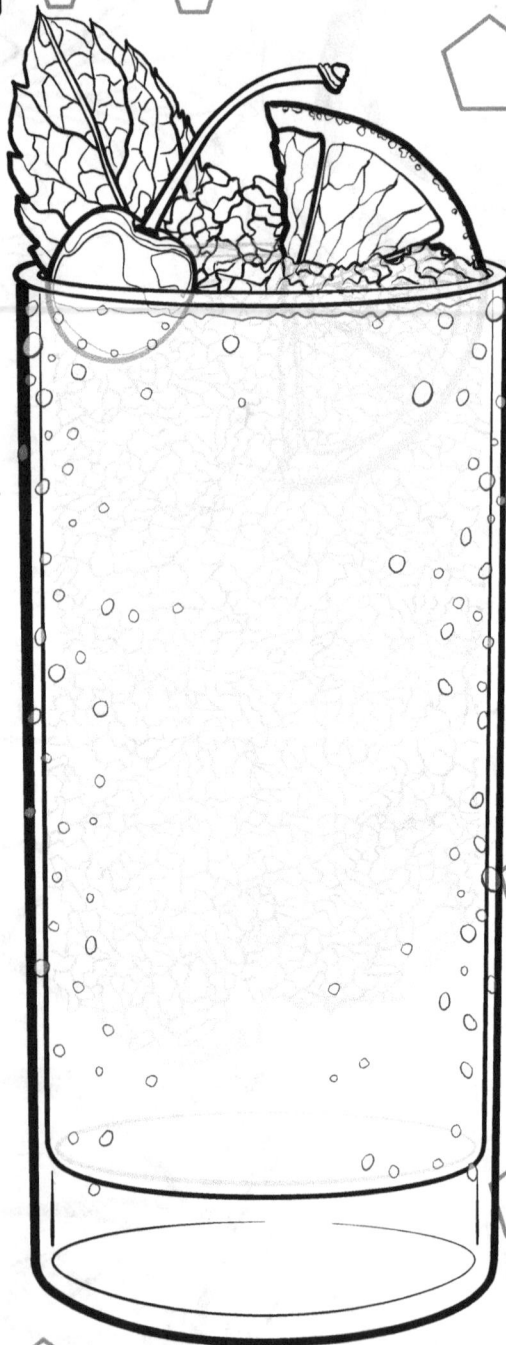

INGREDIENTS:

>>> 3/4 ounce gin
>>> 1/4 ounce Grand Marnier
>>> 1/4 ounce cherry liqueur
>>> 1/4 ounce herbal liqueur
>>> 1 ounce pineapple juice
>>> 1/2 ounce fresh lime juice
>>> 1 dash Angostura bitters
>>> club soda, to top

Garnish: orange slice, cherry

PREPARATION:

Add everything except the club soda to your shaker and shake with ice for 10-15 seconds.
Strain it into a highball glass, and then top with club soda.
Add the cherry and orange slice.

This delightful drink was created in 1915 at a popular watering hole in Singapore.
At that time, it was not dignified for women to drink alcohol in public. They tended to sip fruit drinks (resentfully I would imagine) until one clever rabble rouser, Ngiam Tong Boon, invented the perfect Trojan horse that allowed ladies to drink something that appeared socially acceptable, but was sneakily full of gin!
Necessity is indeed the mother of invention.

Singapore Sling

TEQUILA

Timing: After dinner

Collins glass

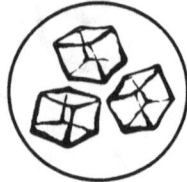
Ice Cubes

Shaker

INGREDIENTS:

>>> 1 1/2 ounce Reposado tequila
>>> 1/2 ounce crème de cassis
>>> 1/2 ounce lime juice,
      freshly squeezed
>>> 3 ounces ginger beer

Garnish: 1 blackberry and 1 lime wheel

PREPARATION:

Add everything except the ginger beer to a shaker with ice and shake for 10-15 seconds.
Strain into Collins or Rocks glass over fresh ice. Top it with the ginger beer. Garnish it with blackberry and lime wheel.

Vamos! El diablo está aquí! Time to get naughty and sinful with El Diablo. This cocktail somehow manages to be both iconic AND overlooked. The earliest reference you'll find is from the Trader Vics catalog from 1946. This is one amazing showcase for tequila. It's sophisticated and incredibly tasty. Don't worry about having leftover creme de cassis, it's a great combo with champagne as well. Also, it's inexpensive and easily found. Just be sure to buy a brand that is made in France with real blackcurrants. What the heck are those? They're only available in Europe but it's a common berry there.

EL DiabLo

Timing: After dinner

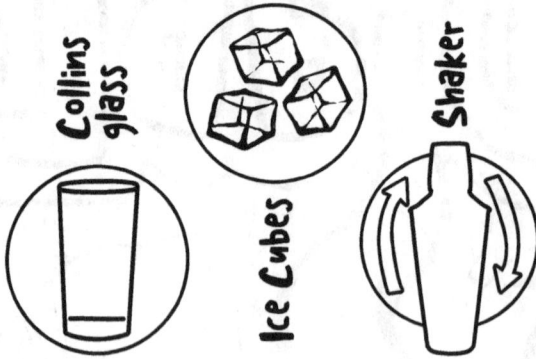

Collins glass

Ice Cubes

Shaker

INGREDIENTS:

>>> 2 oz Gin
>>> 1 oz Fresh lemon juice
>>> 3/4 oz Simple syrup
>>> 1 Egg white
>>> 1 oz Club soda

Garnish: Nutmeg

PREPARATION:

Add everything but the club soda to your shaker and shake without ice for 10 seconds. Toss in 3 or 4 ice cubes and shake for another 10 seconds. Strain into chilled Collins glass and then top with the club soda.

From the heyday of cocktail culture, the Gin Fizz has been around since 1882. I can't really express what's so cool and hip about this drink better than old literature from those early years. From Rex Beach's 1911 novel The Ne'er-Do-Well, Rex deftly writes that the Gin Fizz is "...sweeter than a maiden's smile, more intoxicating than a kiss." And even more compelling, from a 1907 book the Slim Princess... "Do you mean to say that you never heard of a gin fizz?" the author goes on to say, "All the ingredients within reach, simply waiting to be introduced to each other, and you have been holding them apart. You ought to be ashamed of yourself!" If that doesn't make you thirsty, I don't know what will!

Gin Fizz

WINE

Timing: After dinner

Red wine glass

Ice Cubes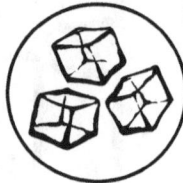

Stir

INGREDIENTS:

>>> 1 bottle dry red wine, like Rioja
>>> 1/2 cup brandy
>>> 1/2 cup orange juice
>>> 2 Tbsp sugar
>>> 1 orange, cut into wedges
>>> 1 apple, cored and diced
>>> 1 lemon, cut into wedges

Garnish: orange wheel

PREPARATION:

In a pitcher, add the oranges, apples, lemon, and sugar, and muddle and mash for 30 seconds.
Add in the orange juice and brandy and keep muddling for another 30 seconds.
Add in the red wine, then stir, then add ice and now serve in red wine glasses.

A marvelous spiked punch, we have the Spanish and Portugese to thank for this drink. It's name literally means bloodletting in Spanish or simply blood in Portugese (sangre). Yikes! It was first introduced to the US at the 1964 World's Fair. It's funny how many cocktails debuted at World Fairs. It's really too bad we don't have them in the US anymore.

WHISKEY

Timing: all day

Mug glass

INGREDIENTS:

- >>> boiling water, to fill a mug
- >>> 4 cloves
- >>> 1 cinnamon stick
- >>> 1 lemon peel or wheel
- >>> 2 tsp Demerara sugar or brown sugar
- >>> Pinch of nutmeg
- >>> 1/4 ounce fresh lemon juice
- >>> 2 ounces bourbon, whiskey, or scotch
- >>> Drizzle of honey, to taste

garnish: cinnamon stick, lemon

PREPARATION:

Fill your coffee mug with the boiling water and then let cool for a minute. While cooling, poke the cloves into the lemon wheel or peel and put aside. Empty your mug and then fill up halfway with new fresh boiling water.

Add in the sugar and then stir up to dissolve. Add in the lemon wheel or peel with cloves and stir. Add the pinch of nutmeg and the cinnamon stick. Add in the whiskey or whatever liquor you use and the lemon juice, and stir. Add a drizzle of honey to sweeten.

Originally created to make raw scotch drinkable in 18th century Scotland, this drink has become a go to for cold and flu sufferers. If you have to be sick, at least be tipsy. Seriously though, hot toddies can really help. Inhaling the steam can help clear nasal passages. The honey and the lemon are also well known for their flu fighting capabilities. And finally, bourbon is a natural decongestant that dilates blood vessels. But don't feel like you have to wait to be sick to enjoy!

Hot Toddy

VODKA

Timing: After dinner

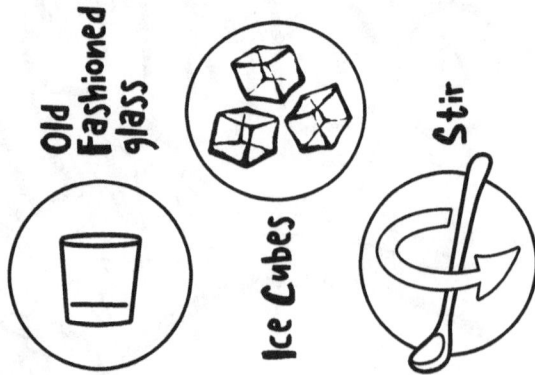

Old Fashioned glass

Ice Cubes

Stir

INGREDIENTS:

>>> 2 ounces vodka
>>> 1 ounce Kahlúa
>>> 1 splash heavy cream

garnish: chocolate straw

PREPARATION:

Pour vodka and Kahlúa into an Old Fashioned glass over ice.
Top with heavy cream and then stir.

If you've never had one of these, of course you've been very un-Duuude... Interestingly, this versatile concoction has no connection at all to Russia other than the vodka.

It is an alternative to the much less popular Black Russian, created by a bartender in Brussels in the 1940's to honor the esteemed American ambassador to Luxembourg.

Belgium, America, Luxembourg, nowhere in the origin story were there any Russians.

RUM

Timing: After dinner

Hurricane glass

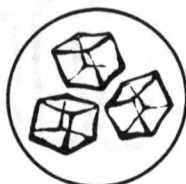
Ice Cubes

Stir

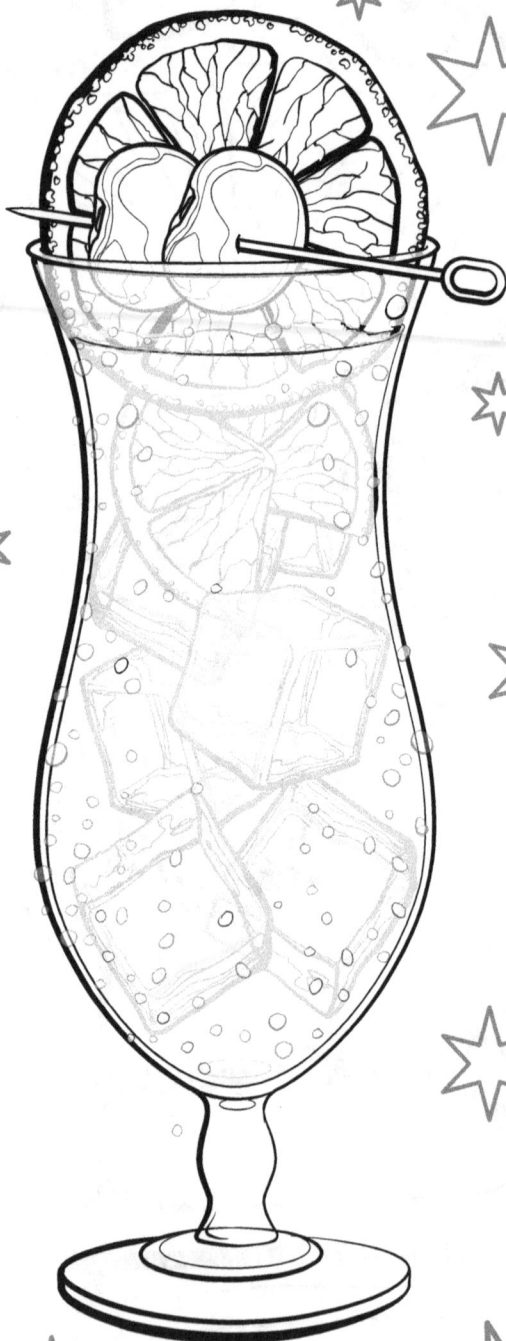

INGREDIENTS:

>>> 2 ounces light rum
>>> 2 ounces dark rum
>>> 1 ounce fresh lime juice
>>> 1 ounce fresh orange juice
>>> 1/2 ounce passion fruit purée
>>> 1/2 ounce simple syrup
>>> 1 barspoon or 10 ml grenadine

Garnish: orange wheel, preserved cherry

PREPARATION:

Add everything to a shaker and shake for 10-15 seconds.
Strain into your large hurricane glass over fresh ice. (For sauntering around like you're in the French Quarter, use a plastic cup)
Garnish with a preserved cherry and half an orange wheel on the rim.

If you've ever been to the New Orleans French Quarter, you know all about this cocktail. Surprisingly, despite New Orleans' history with hurricane weather events, this drink gets its name from the glass it is typically served in which resembles a hurricane lamp.
It was created in the 40's after WWII when rum was plentiful and whiskey and bourbon were both in short supply. Bartenders needed a way to sell all of that rum! This tasty drink did the trick and still does.

HURRICANE

Timing: All day

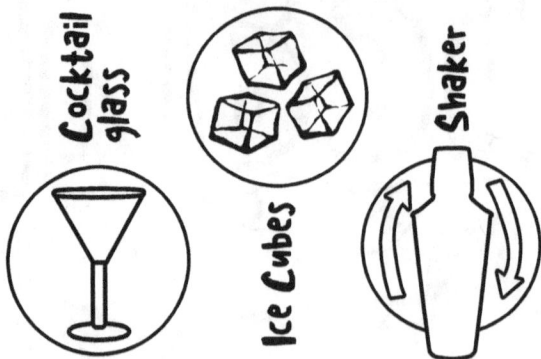

Cocktail glass

Ice Cubes

Shaker

INGREDIENTS:

>>> 1 1/2 oz Citrus vodka
>>> 1 oz Cointreau
>>> 1/2 oz Fresh lime juice
>>> 1 dash Cranberry juice

Garnish: Lime wedge

PREPARATION:

Add everything to a shaker with ice and shake for 10-15 seconds.
Strain into a chilled martini glass.
Garnish with lime wedge.

The Cosmo doesn't have the storied history that many of our other popular cocktails do, but it sure roared into prominence during the Sex and the City years.

An enterprising bartender in Miami gets credited with this one in the 70's. Her customers wanted something that looked as sophisticated as the martini but was sweet instead of sour.

Served in a martini glass with just the right amount of cranberry juice...and a fun time was had by all.

But it didn't truly take off until Carrie Bradshaw popularized the drink in the 90s.

Cosmopolitan

BOURBON

Timing: Before Lunch

 Cocktail glass

 Ice Cube to cool down

 Stir

INGREDIENTS:

>>> 2 oz bourbon or whiskey
>>> 1 oz sweet vermouth
>>> 1 dash Orange bitters
>>> 1 dash Angostura bitters
>>> 1 barspoon Gum syrup

Garnish: Lemon twist or cherry

PREPARATION:

Add everything into a mixing glass, starting with the bitters, and then top with ice.
Stir until well chilled and strain into a chilled cocktail (or coupe) glass.
Squeeze lemon twist over the glass, then drop it in, or just use a cherry.

The origins of the Manhattan have in recent years been diagnosed as a complete myth. It was long believed to have been created at a party at the famed Manhattan Club in NYC in the early 1880's that was hosted by Lady Randolph Churchill, the mother of Winston. While that's a fun story, it's slightly problematic in that she wasn't in New York or even the US at the time. The Manhattan Club still claims this cocktail as their own which could very well still be true. Winston Churchill ended up preferring champagne to cocktails anyway.

BOURBON

Timing: Mid-afternoon

Old Fashioned glass

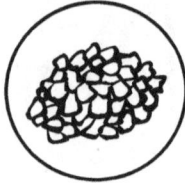
Crushed Ice

Stir

INGREDIENTS:

>>> 1/4 ounce simple syrup
>>> 8 mint leaves
>>> 2 ounces of your favorite bourbon

Garnish: mint leaves

PREPARATION:

In an Old fashioned glass (or Julep cup), delicately muddle or smush the mint together with the syrup.
Add in your bourbon and then tightly pack in crushed ice.
Stir until the outside of your cup is frosted. Top with some more crushed ice if needed.
Smack a mint sprig onto a hard surface like the back of your hand to release the oils and aroma and garnish.

In 1803, the Mint Julep was described in a book as a drink "...taken by Virginians of a morning."
Probably not a bad way to start a day. It has since become the official drink of the Kentucky Derby which ordinarily results in over 120,000 Mint Juleps served at Churchill Downs over every Kentucky Derby weekend. Pandemic years being the exception of course.

Mint Julep

VODKA

Timing: After dinner

Highball glass

Ice Cubes

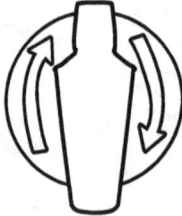
Shaker

INGREDIENTS:

>>> 2 ounces vodka
>>> 3 ounces ginger beer
>>> juice of half a lime

Garnish: lime wheel

PREPARATION:

Add everything into a copper mug (or Highball glass) over ice. Add garnish.

This drink's name is a touch misleading as to its origin. Like so many great cocktails, it was born in Hollywood, not Moscow. And this is the drink that saved Smirnoff vodka. Smirnoff was bought in 1939 for $14,000! Yep, the same price as a used Honda Civic today.

Nobody wanted to drink vodka in those days, everyone was crazy about whiskey. After WWII, the company went all in on the Moscow Mule, which they called the Smirnoff Mule, and it really caught on as it should have. Thanks to this delightful cocktail, Smirnoff sold in 1982 for $1.4 billion. Not too shabby!

MOSCOW MULE

COGNAC

Timing: After dinner

Old Fashioned glass

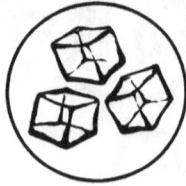
Ice Cubes

Stir

INGREDIENTS:

>>> 5 oz Absinthe
>>> 2 oz Cognac
>>> 5 oz Simple syrup (one part sugar, one part water)
>>> 3 dashes Peychaud's Bitters

Garnish: Lemon twist

PREPARATION:

Rinse a chilled Old Fashioned glass with the absinthe, then fill it up with crushed ice and put aside.
Add everything else to a separate mixing glass, then fill with ice and stir. Discard the ice and any absinthe that's left from your prepared Old Fashioned glass and then strain the drink from the mixing glass into it. Garnish with lemon twist.

America's oldest cocktail...comes to us all the way from 1838, from (of course) the Big Easy's French Quarter. It was originally served in a glass called a Coquetier which is pronounced cock-a-tiay.
The locals in New Orleans claim that this cajun pronunciation is where the word "cocktail" comes from.

Sazerac

TEQUILA

Timing: Before dinner

Margarita or Coupe glass

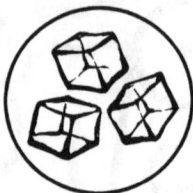
Ice Cubes

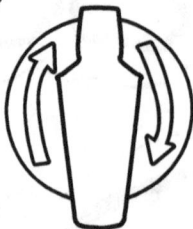
Shaker

INGREDIENTS:

>>> 2 oz Blanco tequila
>>> 1 oz Fresh lime juice
>>> 1/2 oz Orange liqueur
>>> 1/2 oz Agave syrup

Garnish: Lime wheel, Kosher salt

PREPARATION:

Add everything to a shaker with ice and shake for 10-15 seconds.
Strain into Coupe (Margarita) glass (with salt around the rim if you like) over fresh ice. Add your garnish.

Margarita Madness.
Pop Quiz: How many Margaritas are consumed every hour in the US?
It's probably a bit higher in the Summer, but this number makes Margaritas the most popular cocktail in the United States. The answer?
185,000! Every. Hour.
That's what I call a party.

BRANDY

Timing: Before dinner

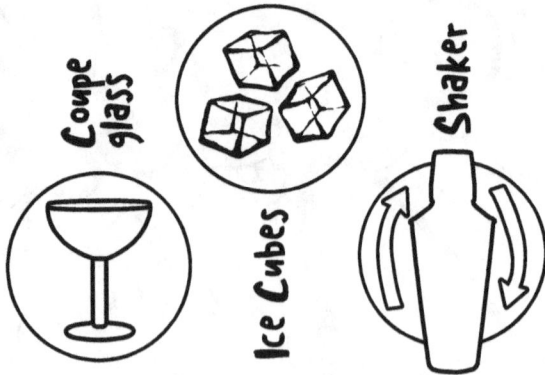

Coupe glass

Ice Cubes

Shaker

INGREDIENTS:

>>> 1 1/2 ounce Brandy or Cognac
>>> 3/4 ounce orange liqueur (Cointreau, Grand Marnier, or Triple Sec)
>>> 3/4 ounce lemon juice, freshly squeezed

Garnish: Sugar Rim & Orange or Lemon Twist

PREPARATION:

Add sugar to the rim of a martini or coupe glass if you want to be fancy.
Shake ingredients for 10-15 seconds in a shaker with ice.
Strain it into your glass.
Garnish with orange or lemon twist

There are lots of arguments about the origin of this classy, timeless drink, but most involve someone needing a pre-dinner drink riding to a bar in a motorbike's sidecar after WWI when that was a more commonplace means of transportation as compared to today.
The sidecar cocktail is still going strong, though I wish the motorcycle sidecar would come back into vogue. But if you know someone who has one, please drink a sidecar in a sidecar and let me know if it's as fun as it sounds.

WHISKEY

Timing: Morning (before Dinner)

Coffee glass or mug

Stir

INGREDIENTS:

>>> 3/4 oz Demerara syrup (one part demerara sugar, one part water)
>>> 1 1/2 oz Irish whiskey
>>> 4 oz Brewed coffee, hot
Heavy cream, lightly whipped

Garnish: Nutmeg

PREPARATION:

Fill a coffee mug or Irish Coffee glass with hot water and then let sit for a couple of minutes to warm up.
Then dump out the water, add in the whiskey, Demerara syrup, and the coffee.
Stir and then top with a layer of heavy cream. You'll want it the width of your thumb.
Garnish with a pinch of ground nutmeg

This soul warming cocktail was invented in 1943 at a small Irish airport for some weary, cold passengers waiting on a delayed flight.
It is that very village of Foynes, Ireland that hosts a yearly Irish Coffee festival which sounds like a fabulous time.
If you're feeling low, this is the drink to turn a day around.
Although the world record Irish Coffee at 15 gallons does seem a bit much.
A dab'll do ye!

RUM

Timing: After dinner

Highball glass

Ice Cubes

Stir

INGREDIENTS:

>>>1 ounce rum
>>>3 ounces Coca-Cola
(from a glass bottle to feel
old school)

Garnish: lime wedge

PREPARATION:

This one is simple.
Add everything to a highball glass
filled with ice.
Garnish with lime wedge.

You're not simply drinking a rum and Coke, that's a Cuba Libre!
One of the most simple drinks for home mixologists, this cocktail was born in 1900 shortly after Cuba had won its independence in the American-Spanish war, when Captain Russell of the US military (stationed in Cuba) ordered a Bacardi and rum with lime and toasted "Por Cuba Libre!" which translates to "For a free Cuba!"
No matter what you're toasting, you can't go wrong with a Cuba Libre.

CuBa LibRe

RUM

Timing: After dinner

Highball glass

Ice Cubes

Stir

INGREDIENTS:

>>> 1/2 oz Cruzan 151 Rum
>>> 1 oz Dark Jamaican Rum
>>> 3/4 oz Fresh Lime Juice
>>> 1 oz White Grapefruit Juice
>>> 1/2 oz Cinnamon Syrup

Garnish: 1 Sprig of Mint

PREPARATION:

Pour everything into your shaker and shake with ice for 10-15 seconds.
Pour unstrained into any tall glass.
Slap the mint to release the oils and aroma and garnish.

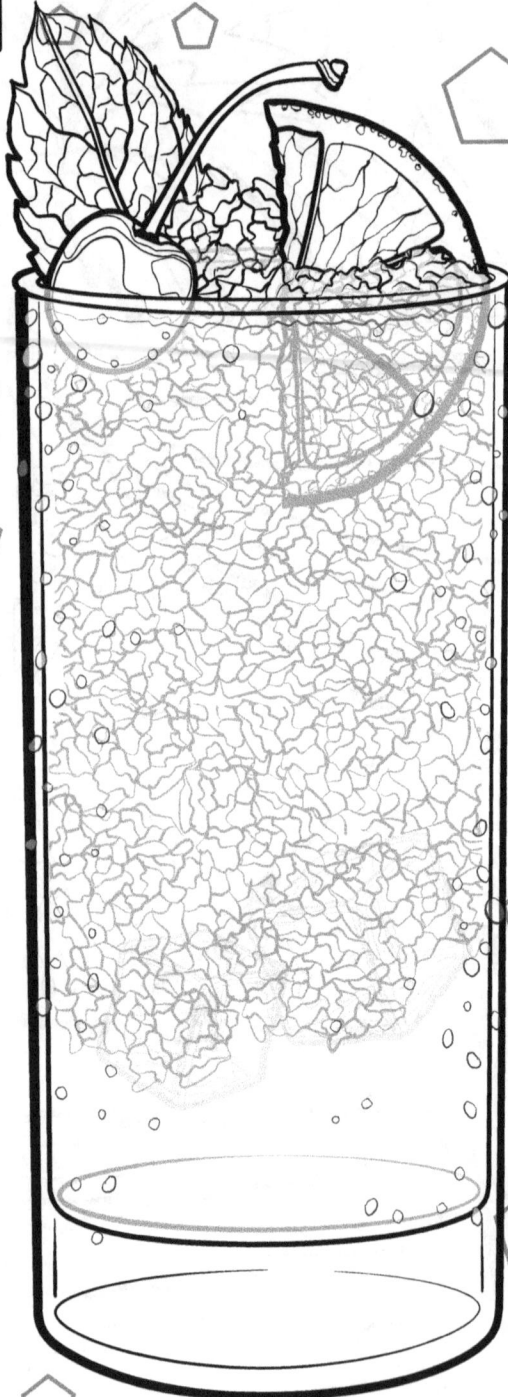

The very essence of Tiki Caribbean drink culture, the Zombie has been referred to as "the mother of all freak drinks".
Potent and not for the faint of heart, it was created by the infamous 'Don the Beachcomber' the grand poobah of Tiki, in 1930's Hollywood, C.A.
In the words of Don himself, the Zombie is the "mender of broken dreams".
Whoah...

Timing: After dinner

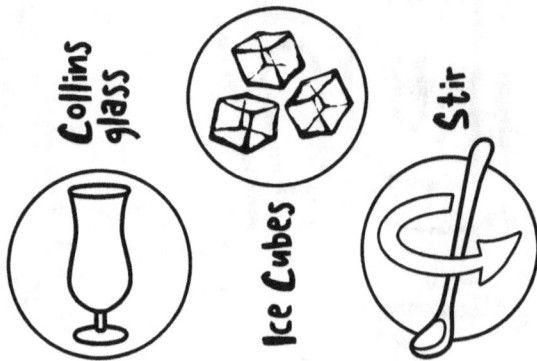

Collins glass

Ice Cubes

Stir

INGREDIENTS:

>>> 2 ounces gin
>>> 1 ounce fresh lemon juice
>>> 1/2 ounce simple syrup
>>> club soda, to top

Garnish: lemon wheel,
maraschino cherry

PREPARATION:

Pour the gin, simple syrup, and lemon juice into a Collins glass.
Then fill with ice, top with club soda, and stir.
Garnish with maraschino cherry and lemon wheel.

The history of this cocktail is full of rascally fun. Picture this. You're a hip, fashionable fixture in the New York bar scene in 1874.
Someone asks you if you've seen Tom Collins. "Who's that?" you ask. They then tell you he was at such and such bar saying bad things about you.
The nerve of this guy! So you head over there only to hear that you just missed him, have a drink.
People all over the city were hitting bar after bar in the search for this fictional, mischief maker.

Tom Collins

COGNAC

Timing: After dinner

Cocktail glass

Ice Cubes

Shaker

INGREDIENTS:

>>> 1 1/2 ounces cognac
>>> 1 ounce dark crème
  de cacao
>>> 1 ounce cream

Garnish: grated nutmeg

PREPARATION:

Add everything to a shaker with ice and shake for 10-15 seconds.
Strain into a chilled cocktail glass or coupe.
Add a small pinch of nutmeg on top.

If you're a Beatles fan, you may already know that the Brandy Alexander was John Lennon's cocktail of choice.
This cocktail, like most, has mysterious origins. But the most commonly accepted is that it was created by a bartender with the last name of Alexander who worked at a famous restaurant in New City in the early 1900's.
That restaurant was Rector's, and it was as upscale as upscale gets. It boasted New York City's very first revolving front door.
Imagine the confusion of humanity encountering that for the first time! Especially after a few Alexanders...

VODKA

Timing: wake up

Collins glass

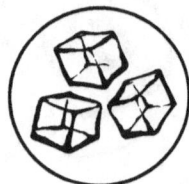

Ice Cubes

Shaker gently

INGREDIENTS:

>>> 1 lemon wedge
>>> 1 lime wedge
>>> 2 ounces vodka
>>> 4 ounces tomato juice
>>> 2 tsp prepared horseradish
>>> 2 dashes Tabasco sauce
>>> 2 dashes worcestershire sauce
>>> 1 pinch celery salt
>>> 1 pinch ground black pepper

Garnish: lime wedge, green olives, parsley sprig, celery stalk

PREPARATION:

Pour the celery salt on a plate. Rub the wet part of a lime or lemon wedge around the outer edge of a Collins glass. Roll or press the lip of the glass in the celery salt until it's fully coated. Fill it up with ice and set it aside. Now squeeze your lime and lemon wedges into your shaker and then drop them in. Add everything else and fill it with ice and shake gently. Strain into your prepared glass. Now add your garnishes. Feel free to go crazy here and add shrimp, bacon, or whatever garnish you can dream up.

A wonderful brunch cocktail, the Bloody Mary was created in Paris during the 1920's. When prohibition ended in the US, the drink became popular there where it was tarted up with horseradish, Tabasco, and lemon juice. Apparently the celery stick became a common garnish in the 1960's when an impatient customer at a Chicago hotel grabbed the first thing he could find to stir his drink. Fortunately this drink became known as the Bloody Mary which seems far more appetizing than its original name, Bucket of Blood.

BLOODY MARY

Timing: After dinner

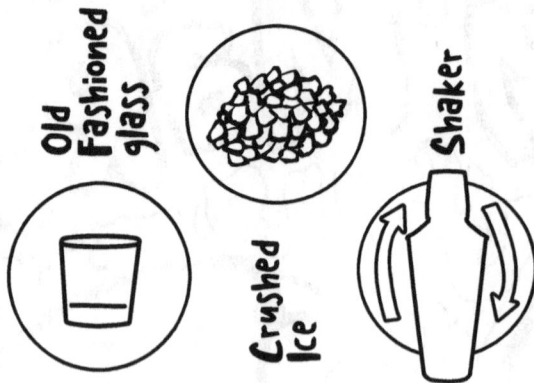

Old Fashioned glass

Crushed Ice

Shaker

INGREDIENTS:

>>> 1 1/2 ounces white rum
>>> 3/4 ounce orange curaçao
>>> 1 ounce fresh lime juice
>>> 1/2 ounce orgeat
>>> 1/2 ounce dark rum

Garnish: lime wheel, mint sprig

PREPARATION:

Add the lime juice, white rum, orgeat, and curacao into your shaker with crushed ice and lightly shake for about 3 seconds.

Pour everything into an Old Fashioned glass. Float the dark rum over the top. (Floating means to hold a spoon upside down over the drink and slowly pour the dark rum onto the spoon.) Garnish with mint sprig and lime wheel.

The clean cut but complex ambassador of Tiki culture.

As the story goes, in a 1930's Hollywood Tiki bar, a Tahitian woman upon tasting this elaborate concoction exclaimed, "Maita'i roa a'e!" which means "out of this world the best!" in Tahitian. A key secret is to use a healthy dose of crushed ice.

Mai Tai

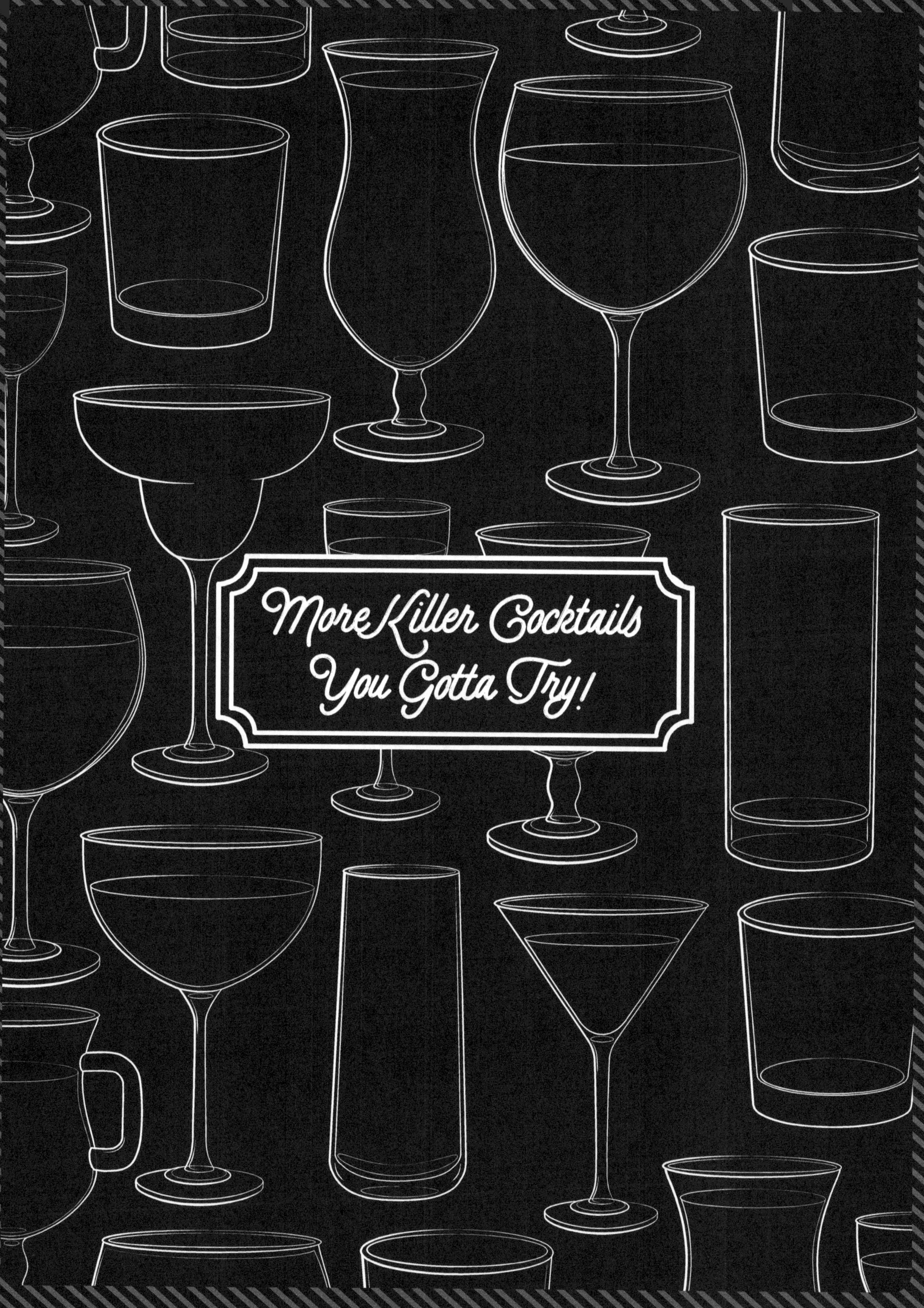
More Killer Cocktails
You Gotta Try!

VODKA

Porn star martini

1 1/2 ounces vanilla-flavored vodka
1/2 ounce passion fruit liqueur
1 ounce passion fruit puree
1/2 ounce lime juice, freshly squeezed
1/2 ounce vanilla simple syrup
2 ounces sparkling wine, chilled
Garnish: 1/2 passion fruit

Add everything except the sparkling wine into your shaker and shake with ice for 10-15 seconds. Then strain into chilled coupe glass and add garnish. Serve with the sparkling wine sidecar on the side.

Blue Hawaii

3/4 ounce vodka
3/4 ounce light rum
1/2 ounce blue curaçao
3 ounces pineapple juice
1 ounce sweet-and-sour mix
Garnish: pineapple wedge

Add all everything into your shaker and shake with ice for 10-15 seconds. You can also blend everything with ice in a blender if you want it frozen. It's good either way.
Then strain into Hurricane glass over fresh crushed ice and add garnish.

Midori Sour

1 ounce Midori
1 ounce Vodka
1/2 ounce Fresh lemon juice
1/2 ounce Fresh lime juice
Soda water, to top
Garnish: Lemon wheel

Add everything but the soda water into a Collins glass over ice and stir.
Then top with soda water and add garnish.

Espresso Martini

2 ounces Vodka
1/2 ounce Simple syrup
1/2 ounce Coffee liqueur
1 ounce Freshly brewed espresso
Garnish: Coffee beans

Add everything to your shaker and shake with ice for 10-15 seconds.
Strain into chilled cocktail glass and garnish with a few coffee beans.

Cucumber, Basil & Lime Gimlet

1 1/2 ounces vodka
2 slices cucumber (1/4-inch slices)
1 1/2 fresh basil leaves
1 ounce lemonade
1/4 ounce lime juice, freshly squeezed
Garnish: basil leaf

Muddle and mash the cucumber and basil in your shaker. Add everything else and shake with ice for 10-15 seconds.
Strain into rocks glass over fresh ice and add garnish.

Lemon Drop

2 ounces Vodka
1/2 ounce Triple sec
1 ounce Simple syrup
1 ounce Fresh lemon juice
Garnish: Sugar rim

Take a cocktail glass and coat rim with sugar and put aside for a few minutes until the sugar has dried. Add everything to your shaker and shake with ice for 10-15 seconds.
Strain into your prepared glass.

Oak Lily

1 1/2 ounces vodka
1/2 ounce orange liqueur
1/2 ounce simple syrup
1/2 ounce lemon juice, freshly squeezed
3 ounces cranberry juice
Garnish: lemon wheel, 2 blackberries on skewer

Add everything to a highball glass.
Add in the ice and then stir.
Add garnish.

Kamikaze

2 ounces Vodka
3/4 ounces Orange liqueur
3/4 ounces Fresh lime juice

Recipe makes two shots.
Add everything into your shaker and shake with ice for 10-15 seconds.
Strain into shot glasses and bottoms up!.

Ruby

1 1/2 ounces vodka
1/2 ounce Aperol
3/4 ounce elderflower liqueur
3/4 ounce freshly squeezed ruby red grapefruit juice
3/4 ounce freshly squeezed lemon juice
1 Tbsp egg white
Garnish: expressed grapefruit twist

Add everything into your shaker and shake without ice. Then add ice and now shake again for 10-15 seconds.
Strain into chilled coupe glass and garnish.

Bloody Caesar

celery salt
1 1/2 ounces vodka
4 ounces Clamato juice
2 dashes Worcestershire sauce
2 dashes Tabasco sauce
prepared horseradish, to taste (optional)
Garnish: cucumber spear, lime wedge, celery stalk

Roll the rim of a tall glass in celery salt so it's good and coated. Fill it with ice and put aside. Add everything else to a mixing glass with ice. Pour it back and forth between that and another mixing glass a couple of times to mix. Strain it into the glass with the salted rim and add garnish.

Transfusion

Concord grape juice, for ice cubes
2 ounces vodka
1/2 ounce ginger syrup
1/2 ounce fresh lime juice
2 ounces club soda
Garnish: concord grapes, crystallized ginger

Start by making grape juice ice cubes and having them ready to go in your freezer.Add the lime juice, vodka, and ginger syrup, into your shaker and shake with ice for 10-15 seconds. Strain it into rocks glass filled with your grape juice ice cubes. Top with club soda and garnish.

French Martini

2 ounces vodka
1 3/4 ounces pineapple juice
1/4 ounce crème de cassis liqueur

Add everything to your shaker and shake with ice for 10-15 seconds.
Strain into chilled martini glass.

GIN

Breakfast Martini

1 spoonful Orange Marmalade
1 ⅔ ounces Gin
1/2 ounce ounces Triple sec
1/2 ounce ounces Lemon juice (freshly squeezed)
Garnish: Orange zest twist

Stir the marmalade in with the gin in your shaker until well mixed.
Add in everything else and shake with ice for 10-15 seconds. Strain into chilled martini glass.

Ramos Gin Fizz

2 ounces gin
1/2 ounce heavy cream
1/2 ounce lemon juice, freshly squeezed
1/2 ounce fresh lime juice, freshly squeezed
3/4 ounce simple syrup
3 dashes orange flower water
1 fresh egg white / Club soda, to top

Add everything except club soda into your shaker and shake without ice for 10 seconds. Then fill up with ice and shake it again for 10-15 seconds. Strain into Collins glass. Pour a dash of club soda from one empty half of the shaker to the other to get the rest of the egg white and pour into your glass.

Monkey Gland

2 ounces gin
1 ounce orange juice
1/4 ounce grenadine
Dash of absinthe
Garnish: orange slice

Swirl a dash of absinthe into a chilled cocktail glass to coat, then dump it out.
Add everything else to your shaker and shake with ice for 10-15 seconds.
Then strain into your prepared cocktail glass and add garnish.

Bebbo

1 1/2 ounces gin
3/4 ounce fresh lemon juice
1/4 ounce fresh blood orange juice
1 ounce honey syrup
Garnish: lemon twist

Add everything into your shaker and shake with ice for 10-15 seconds.
Strain into chilled coupe and garnish.

Vesper Martini

3 ounces gin
1 ounce vodka
1/2 ounce Lillet blanc apéritif
Garnish: lemon twist

Add everything into your mixing glass full of ice and stir until it is well-chilled.
Then strain into chilled martini glass and garnish.

Suffering Bastard

1 ounces Bourbon
1 ounces London dry gin
1/2 ounces Fresh lime juice
2 dashes Angostura bitters
Ginger ale, to top
Garnish: Mint sprig

Add the gin, bourbon, bitters, and lime juice into your shaker and shake with ice for 30 seconds. Strain it into Collins glass over fresh ice and top with ginger ale. Garnish.

Negroni

1 ounce gin
1 ounce Campari
1 ounce sweet vermouth
Garnish: orange peel

Add everything to a mixing glass filled with ice, and stir until it is completely chilled.
Strain into rocks glass over fresh ice and garnish.

Sea Breeze Cooler

1 ounce dry gin
1 ounce apricot brandy
juice of half a lemon
2 dashes grenadine
soda water, to top
Garnish: mint sprig

Add everything except soda water to highball glass over ice and top with the soda water. Garnish.

Hanky Panky

1 1/2 ounces Gin
1 1/2 ounces Sweet vermouth
2 dashes Fernet-Branca
Garnish: Orange twist

Add everything to your mixing glass with ice, then stir.
Strain into chilled martini glass and garnish.

Gin Gimlet

2 1/2 ounces gin
1/2 ounce fresh lime juice
1/2 ounce simple syrup
Garnish: lime wheel

Add everything to your shaker and shake with ice for 10-15 seconds.
Strain into chilled rocks glass over fresh ice and garnish.

Angel Face

1 ounce gin
1 ounce Applejack
1 ounce apricot liqueur
Garnish: Orange peel

Pour everything into your shaker and shake with ice for 10-15 seconds.
Strain into chilled martini glass and add garnish.

Aviation

2 ounces gin
1/2 ounce maraschino liqueur
1/2 ounce crème de violette or crème yvette
3/4 ounce fresh lemon juice
Garnish: brandied cherry

Add everything into your shaker and shake with ice for 10-15 seconds.
Strain into chilled martini glass and add garnish.

GIN

French 75

1 ounce gin
1/2 ounce fresh lemon juice
1/2 ounce simple syrup
3 ounces Champagne or other sparkling wine
Garnish: lemon twist

Add everything but the Champagne to your shaker and shake with ice for 10-15 seconds. Strain into Champagne flute and top with Champagne.
Add garnish.

Southside

2 oz Gin
1 oz Fresh lemon juice
5 Mint leaves
1 oz Simple syrup
Garnish: Mint sprig, Lemon twist

Muddle and mash the mint with the lemon juice in your shaker.
Add everything else and shake with ice for 10-15 seconds. Strain into chilled cocktail glass with stem and garnish.

RUM

Daiquiri

2 ounces light rum
1 ounce fresh lime juice
3/4 ounce demerara sugar syrup
Garnish: lime twist

Add everything into your shaker and shake with ice for 30 seconds or blend everything with ice. Strain into chilled coupe and garnish.

Banana Daiquiri

2 ounces aged rum
1/2 ounce crème de banane liqueur
1 ounce fresh lime juice
1/4 ounce Demerara simple syrup
Garnish: banana slice

Add everything into your shaker and shake with ice for 30 seconds or blend it with ice. Strain into chilled coupe and garnish.

Painkiller

2 ounces rum
4 ounces pineapple juice
1 ounce orange juice
1 ounce cream of coconut
Garnish: grated nutmeg, pineapple wedge

Add everything into your shaker and shake with ice for 10-15 seconds.
Strain into hurricane glass over crushed ice and garnish.

Rum Swizzle

4 ounces dark rum
4 ounces gold rum
8 oz Pineapple juice
8 oz Orange juice
3/4 oz Grenadine
6 dashes Angostura bitters
Garnish: Orange slice, Pineapple cube, Cherry

Fill up a pitcher about a third with crushed ice, and add in all ingredients. Stir hard until frothing or shake it all in a large shaker, and then strain it into four rocks glasses over fresh ice and garnish.

Miami Vice

2 ounces rum, divided
1 cup strawberries, chopped with stems removed
1 ounce fresh lime juice
1/2 ounce simple syrup
2 ounces cream of coconut
2 ounces pineapple juice
Garnish: pineapple slice

In your blender, add 1 ounce of rum, the lime juice, the simple syrup, the strawberries, and a cup of crushed ice. Then blend until smooth. Pour into hurricane glass and put in your freezer. Wash your blender thoroughly. Then in your blender, add the final ounce of rum, the pineapple juice, the cream of coconut, and a cup of crushed ice. Blend until smooth. Pour into your prepared hurricane glass with the Strawberry Daiquiri mix and garnish.

Rum Old Fashioned

2 ounces dark rum
1 bar spoon Demerara syrup
1 bar spoon Allspice dram
2 dashes orange bitters
2 dashes Angostura bitters
Garnish: orange twist

Stir everything in a rocks glass until it is all well chilled and add garnish.

Rum Runner

1 ounce Spiced Rum
1 ounce White Rum
1/2 ounce Crème de Banana Liqueur
1/2 ounce Blackberry Liqueur (or Crème de Cassis)
1 ounce Orange Juice
1 ounce Pineapple Juice
1 ounce Lime Juice
1/2 ounce Grenadine
Garnish: Maraschino Cherries, Orange Slices, Lime Slices, Pineapple Wedges

Add everything to your shaker and shake with ice for 10-15 seconds.
Strain into Collins glass over fresh ice and garnish.

Canchanchara

1 1/2 ounce white rum
Juice of 1 lime
1/2 ounce honey syrup
1 splash soda water
Garnish: lime wedge

Add the rum, honey syrup and lime juice into your shaker and shake with ice for 10-15 seconds. Strain into glass mug over fresh ice and top with a dash of soda water. Add garnish.

Man o' War

2 ounces bourbon
1 ounce orange curaçao or triple sec
1/2 ounce sweet vermouth
1/2 ounce lemon juice, freshly squeezed
Garnish: lemon peel, brandied cherry

Add everything into your shaker and shake with ice for 10-15 seconds.
Strain into chilled Rocks glass and garnish.

Scofflaw

2 ounces bourbon or rye whiskey
1 ounce dry vermouth
1/4 ounce fresh lemon juice
1 to 2 dashes grenadine
1 dash orange bitters

Add everything into your shaker and shake with ice for 10-15 seconds.
Strain into chilled Rocks glass.

BOURBON

Amaretto Sour

1 1/2 ounces amaretto liqueur
3/4 ounce bourbon
1 ounce lemon juice, freshly squeezed
1 teaspoon rich simple syrup
1/2 ounce egg white, beaten
Garnish: lemon twist, 2 skewered brandied cherries

Add everything into your shaker and shake without ice. Then add ice and shake again for 10-15 seconds. Strain into Rocks glass over fresh ice and garnish.

Egg Nog

2 eggs, separated
1/4 cup sugar, divided
4 ounces rum, bourbon or brandy
10 ounces whole milk
4 ounces heavy cream
Garnish: grated nutmeg

Beat together the egg yolks and the sugar until nice and fluffy in a large bowl. Then stir in the heavy cream, milk, and 4 ounces of your favorite spirit. In another bowl, beat the egg whites until fluffy. Fold the egg whites into the yolk mix and serve.

Lion's Tail

2 ounces bourbon
4 dashes Angostura bitters
1/2 ounce fresh lime juice
1/2 ounce simple syrup
1/2 ounce allspice dram
Garnish: orange peel

Add everything into your shaker and shake with ice for 10-15 seconds.
Strain into rocks glass or coupe and garnish

Gold Rush

2 ounces bourbon
1 ounce honey syrup
3/4 ounce fresh lemon juice
Garnish: lemon peel

Add everything into your shaker and shake with ice for 30 seconds.
Then strain into chilled rocks glass with one ice cube and garnish.

The Godfather

2 ounces Blended scotch or bourbon
1/4 ounce Amaretto

Pour ingredients over ice into mixing glass and stir for 30 seconds until chilled.
Strain into a rocks glass over fresh ice.

Paper Plane

3/4 ounce bourbon
3/4 ounce Aperol
3/4 ounce Amaro Nonino Quintessentia
3/4 ounce fresh lemon juice

Add everything to your shaker and shake with ice for 10-15 seconds.
Strain into coupe.

Penicillin

2 ounces scotch
3/4 ounce lemon juice, freshly squeezed
3/4 ounce honey-ginger syrup*
1/4 ounce single malt scotch
Garnish: candied ginger

Add the scotch, syrup and juice into your shaker and shake with ice for 10-15 seconds.
Strain into rocks glass over fresh ice and top with single malt scotch.
Add garnish.

Whiskey Mac

1 1/2 ounce blended scotch
1 ounce green ginger wine

Pour scotch and ginger wine over ice into rocks glass and stir.

Drunk Uncle

1 1/2 ounces scotch
3/4 ounce bianco vermouth
3/4 ounce amaro
Garnish: Grapefruit twist

Add everything to a mixing glass over ice and stir until chilled.
Then strain into chilled coupe glass and garnish.

Rusty Nail

1 1/2 ounces Scotch
3/4 ounces Drambuie

Add scotch and Drambuie over ice into a rocks glass and stir.

Rob Roy

2 ounces Scotch
3/4 ounces Sweet vermouth
3 dashes Angostura bitters
Garnish: Brandied cherry

Add everything over ice into mixing glass and stir. Then strain into chilled cocktail glass and garnish.

Presbyterian

2 ounces scotch
ginger ale
club soda

Pour the scotch over ice into Collins glass and then top with ginger ale and club soda equally.

WHISKEY

Whiskey Sour

2 ounces bourbon
3/4 ounce fresh lemon juice
1/2 ounce simple syrup
1/2 ounce egg white
Garnish: Angostura bitters

Add everything into your shaker and dry shake for 10 seconds with no ice.
Then add ice and shake again for 10-15 seconds.
Strain into coupe glass.
Garnish with 3-4 drops of Angostura bitters

Monte Carlo

2 ounces rye whiskey
1/2 ounce Bénédictine
1 dash Angostura bitters

Add everything to a mixing glass over ice and stir until chilled (about 30 seconds).
Then strain into chilled rocks glass with an ice cube.

Alabama Slammer

1 ounce Southern Comfort
1 ounce Sloe gin
1 ounce Amaretto
2 ounces Fresh orange juice
Garnish: Orange wedge

Add everything into your shaker and shake with ice for 10-15 seconds.
Then strain over fresh ice into highball glass and garnish.

Irish Maid

2 slices Cucumber (1/4-inch slices)
2 ounces Irish whiskey
1/2 ounce elderflower liqueur.
3/4 ounce Fresh lemon juice
3/4 ounce Simple syrup
Garnish: Cucumber slice

Muddle and mash the cucumber slices at the bottom of your shaker. Then add everything else with ice and shake for 10-15 seconds. Strain over ice into chilled rocks glass and garnish.

Washington Apple

1 ounce Canadian whisky
1 ounce sour apple schnapps
1 ounce cranberry juice
Garnish: 1 apple slice

Add everything into your shaker and shake with ice for 10-15 seconds.
Strain into coupe glass and garnish

John Collins

2 ounces bourbon whiskey
1 ounce lemon juice
1 teaspoon simple syrup
2 cups ice, divided
2 fluid ounces club soda
Garnish: orange slice, lemon slice, maraschino cherry

Add the bourbon, the lemon juice, and the simple syrup into your shaker and shake with ice for 10-15 seconds. Strain into Collins glass and then add ice, top with club soda, and stir. Add garnish.

Tequila Sunrise

2 ounces white tequila
4 ounces orange juice, freshly squeezed
1/4 ounce grenadine
Garnish: orange slice, cherry

Pour the tequila and the orange juice into a chilled glass over ice.
Top with grenadine, which sinks. This creates a layering effect. Garnish and serve.

Mezcal Mule

3 cucumber slices
3/4 ounce lime juice, freshly squeezed
1 1/2 ounces Sombra mezcal
3/4 ounce Boiron passion fruit purée
1/2 ounce agave nectar
ginger beer, to top
Garnish: cucumber slice, candied ginger, pinch of chile powder

Muddle and mash the cucumber slices with the lime juice at the bottom of your shaker.
Add in everything else with ice (except for the ginger beer) and shake for 10-15 seconds.
Then strain over ice into rocks glass and top with ginger beer. Garnish and serve.

Devil's Margarita

1 1/2 ounce blanco tequila
1 ounce lime juice, freshly squeezed
3/4 ounce simple syrup
1/2 ounce red wine
Garnish: lime wheel

Add the tequila, syrup and lime juice with ice to your shaker and shake for 30 seconds.
Then strain into a glass.
Top with the red wine and garnish.

Tequila Mockingbird

1 Jalapeño pepper slice
3 Watermelon cubes (about ⅓ cup)
2 ounces Silver tequila
3/4 ounces Fresh lime juice
3/4 ounces Agave syrup

Muddle and mash the watermelon and jalapeño at the bottom of your shaker. Add in everything else with ice and shake for 10-15 seconds.
Strain over fresh ice into rocks glass.

Paloma

2 ounces tequila
1/2 ounce fresh lime juice
grapefruit soda, to top
Garnish: lime wheel

Pour in the lime juice and tequila over ice into a Collins glass.
Then top with the grapefruit soda and stir.

Envy Cocktail

1 1/2 ounces silver tequila
1 ounce blue curaçao
1/2 ounce pineapple juice
Garnish: maraschino cherry

Add the tequila, the blue curacao, and the pineapple juice to your shaker and shake with ice for 10-15 seconds.
Strain into chilled martini glass over fresh ice and garnish.

COGNAC

Vieux Carré

4 dashes pimento aromatic bitters
2 tsp Bénédictine
3/4 oz Sweet vermouth
3/4 oz Cognac
3/4 oz rye whiskey
Garnish: Maraschino cherry or lemon peel

Stir everything in a mixing glass with ice for 30 seconds. Strain into rocks glass and add garnish.

Between the Sheets

1 oz Cognac
1 oz Triple sec
1 oz Light rum
1/4 oz Fresh lemon juice
Garnish: Flamed orange peel

Add everything to your shaker and shake with ice for 10-15 seconds.
Strain into chilled martini glass.
Flame orange peel over the drink, then discard.

French Connection

1 1/2 ounces cognac
1 ounce amaretto

Pour everything over ice into rocks glass and stir.

American Beauty

1 1/2 ounces Cognac
1/4 ounce crème de menthe
1/4 ounce Simple Syrup
1 ounce fresh orange juice
1/2 ounce grenadine
1/4 ounce tawny port
Garnish: 1 mint sprig

Add everything but the port to your shaker and shake with ice for 10-15 seconds.
Then add the port while stirring and garnish.

OTHER

Grasshopper

1 oz Green crème de menthe
1 oz White crème de cacao
2 oz Heavy cream
Garnish: Fresh nutmeg

Add everything to your shaker and shake with ice for 10-15 seconds.
Strain into chilled martini glass or coupe and add a pinch of fresh nutmeg as a garnish.

Americano

1 1/2 ounces Campari
1 1/2 ounces sweet vermouth
1 splash club soda
Garnish: orange twist

Pour Campari and vermouth over ice into a rocks glass and top with club soda. .
Add the garnish.

Bellini

1 1/2 oz fresh white peach purée
prosecco, chilled
Garnish: peach slice

Pour peach purée into Champagne flute.
Fill it up with prosecco and add garnish.

Aperol Spritz

3 ounces prosecco
2 ounces Aperol
1 ounce soda water
Garnish: orange wheel

Add everything to a wine glass over ice and stir.
Add garnish.

Tropical Lust

1 1/2 oz sloe gin (or Gin)
1/2 oz peach liqueur
1/2 oz Midori melon liqueur
Pineapple Juice
1 oz vodka

Pour the gin and vodka over ice into a rocks or
Collins glass.
Nearly fill it up with the pineapple juice and then
add the peach and melon liqueurs. Also makes a
good frozen drink by blending with ice.

Tia Mia

1 ounce Mezcal
1 ounce Amber Rum
3/4 ounce Lime Juice
1/2 ounce Dry Curaçao
1/2 ounce Orgeat
Garnish: Mint sprig, Lime wheel

Add everything to your shaker and shake with
ice for 10-15 seconds.
Strain over fresh crushed ice in a chilled rocks
glass and garnish.

Coco Cabana

1 oz coconut rum
 ounce banana liqueur
 ounce melon liqueur, such as Midori
4 ounces pineapple juice
splash grenadine
splash club soda

Add the coconut rum, banana liqueur, melon
liqueur, and pineapple juice to your shaker and
shake with ice for 10-15 seconds.
Strain into Collins glass over fresh ice and top
with grenadine and club soda.

Pink Flamingo

2 ounces rum
3/4 ounce fresh lime juice
3 ounces pink grapefruit soda
Garnish: 1 lime wheel or long lime twist

Pour the rum and the lime juice into your shaker
and shake with ice for 10-15 seconds.
Strain into a rocks glass over fresh ice and top
with the grapefruit soda and add garnish.

www.ingramcontent.com/pod-product-compliance
Lightning Source LLC
Chambersburg PA
CBHW081636040426
42449CB00014B/3331